GERMANY

A Comprehensive Guide to Explore the Trails of
Germany - (Bavarian Alps, Black Forest, Saxon
Switzerland National Park, Harz National Park,
Romantic Road, Moselle and Rhine Valleys)

CURZIO MANNA

TABLE OF CONTENTS

INTRODUCTION TO GERMANY AS A HIKING DESTINATION

Germany, with its diverse landscapes, has emerged as a refuge for hikers. The nation offers hikers a broad variety of experiences, from the rough terrains of the Bavarian Alps to the charming paths of the Black Forest. Germany encourages outdoor travelers to discover its natural beauties with its well-maintained network of hiking pathways. Germany is a perfect vacation for individuals seeking both calm and action, thanks to its scenic beauty and expertly maintained infrastructure.

Germany's geographical variety adds greatly to its allure. The Bavarian Alps, with their towering peaks and alpine meadows, provide a stunning exhibition of nature's majesty. The mysterious Black Forest enchants with its lush greenery and twisting pathways. The variety of sceneries, from rolling hills to beautiful lakes, ensures that every hiker will find a track that suits their interests.

Importance of Hiking in German Culture

Hiking is strongly ingrained in Germany's cultural fiber. It is more than just a sport; it is a way of life. Germans have a strong connection to nature, and hiking allows them to immerse themselves in the country's natural beauty. Walking is a centuries-old tradition, with a multitude of well-maintained hiking roads and trails crisscrossing the whole country.

The way hiking is incorporated into Germany's cultural character demonstrates the country's commitment to conserving its natural beauty. Families, friends, and lone hikers all go to the trails in search of the quiet that the trails provide. The wide network of hiking organizations and activities reflects the social spirit, promoting the concept that hiking is a shared experience that creates a feeling of community rather than merely a physical exercise.

Target Audience for the Hiking Guide

This hiking guide is created for a wide range of people with varied degrees of hiking expertise and interests. This book gives essential insights and ideas whether you are a newbie hiker looking to explore moderate, family-friendly paths or an experienced explorer looking for the challenge of alpine peaks.

This book caters to families searching for easy and pleasurable treks, lone travelers seeking quiet, and seasoned hikers wanting the excitement of conquering difficult terrains. It is intended to be a complete resource, including not just route suggestions but also cultural and gastronomic insights into hiking in Germany. This book seeks to inspire and support a wonderful hiking experience for everyone by adapting the material to the individual requirements and interests of various groups.

In the pages that follow, we'll go further into the complexities of Germany's hiking environment, examining the finest paths, offering practical advice, and unraveling the cultural tapestry that makes hiking in Germany such a rewarding experience. Lace up your boots, take a deep breath of the fresh mountain air, and set off on a trek into the heart of Germany's intriguing hiking routes.

ESSENTIAL INFORMATION

Geographical overview

1. Diverse Landscapes and Regions

Germany, located in the center of Europe, has a stunning range of landscapes that enchant the senses and provide a plethora of hiking options. The country is a patchwork of geographical delights, with each area displaying a distinct combination of topography, climate, and natural beauty.

The Bavarian Alps dominate the scenery, beginning in the south and including snow-capped peaks, alpine meadows, and gorgeous lakes. This area has demanding routes for experienced mountaineers as well as peaceful pathways for those looking for a more pleasant hiking experience. The Black Forest expands westward, with its lush trees, gushing waterfalls, and rolling hills. Hikers are treated to a storybook environment, with routes winding through old trees and offering panoramic views.

As we go north, the landscape changes to rolling hills and river valleys. The Rhine Valley, with its vineyard-covered hills, offers a unique hiking experience that combines nature and cultural richness. The Harz Mountains in the east are a combination of lush woods, mountainous terrain, and lovely medieval villages, with a broad selection of paths ideal for all ability levels.

Coastal areas around the North and Baltic Seas reveal a particular aspect of the German landscape. The Wadden Sea, a UNESCO World Heritage site, is known for its tidal flats and diverse habitats. Hiking along the shore is a rejuvenating experience, with views of the water going all the way to the horizon.

2. Popular Hiking Locations

Germany's image as a hiking paradise is well-deserved, due to popular hiking locations that appeal to a wide range of interests. The famed Zugspitze, Germany's tallest summit, attracts experienced mountaineers and climbers. The Allgäu area of the Alps, with its picturesque scenery, is a popular destination for visitors seeking a balance of adventure and tranquility.

The Black Forest stretches across southwest Germany and is famous for its large network of hiking routes. The Westweg, a long-distance route in Germany, leads hikers into the heart of the Black Forest, exhibiting its breathtaking splendor.

Despite its name, Saxon Switzerland National Park is situated in eastern Germany and provides a unique hiking experience. The park, which is distinguished by spectacular sandstone formations and steep gorges, offers tough hikes among magnificent landscapes.

Harz National Park in central Germany is a nature lover's paradise. The Harz Mountains, with their different habitats, including thick woods and high plateaus, provide opportunities for both peaceful strolls and strenuous climbs.

Another popular hiking site is the Moselle Valley, which runs along the Moselle River. This area, known for its vineyards, picturesque towns, and old castles, provides a mix of cultural and natural attractions along its hiking paths.

These famous hiking regions serve as entry points to Germany's natural beauties, encouraging hikers to discover the different landscapes that distinguish this enthralling nation. Whether you're attracted to the alpine heights, mysterious woods, or tranquil river valleys, Germany has a hiking experience to suit any adventurer's preferences.

Climate and Best Hiking Season

Hiking in Germany is a lovely experience, influenced by the country's moderate climate, which provides a variety of seasonal landscapes. Understanding seasonal fluctuations and taking weather conditions into account is essential for planning a successful and pleasant hiking experience.

Seasonal Changes

Germany has four different seasons, each with its allure for hikers:

- **Spring (March to May):** As flowers blossom and the countryside turns into a tapestry of hues, spring pours new life into the landscapes. Temperatures gradually climb, making it excellent for lower-altitude walks and enjoying wildflower meadows. The waking of animals in the spring also provides an opportunity for nature lovers to see species along the paths.

- **Summer (June to August):** Summer brings mild weather, longer days, and a plethora of outdoor activities. Hiking is popular throughout this season in all places, from the alpine peaks to the beach routes. Prepare for busier trails, particularly in famous tourist areas. The Alps and other hilly locations are appealing because they give refuge from the heat.

- **Autumn (September to November):** The foliage turns into a palette of reds, oranges, and yellows, creating a visual spectacular. The weather continues pleasant, and the fresh air adds to the trekking experience. Trails in the Black Forest and other forested regions provide a spectacular display of October hues. Furthermore, since visitor numbers are lower during this season, trekking is more peaceful.

- **Winter (December to February):** Winter turns Germany into a winter paradise, particularly in the south. While lower-altitude pathways may be snow-covered, higher-altitude places become popular for winter activities such as snowshoeing. With festive markets and lighting, the Christmas season gives a beautiful touch to many hiking regions.

Weather Considerations

- **Temperature:** Due to Germany's moderate climate, temperatures may fluctuate greatly throughout the year. Summers are typically temperate to warm, with temperatures ranging from 20 to 30 degrees Celsius (68 to 86 degrees Fahrenheit) throughout the day. Winters may be very cold, with temperatures often falling below freezing, particularly in mountainous areas.

- **Rainfall:** Rain is a possibility all year, so hikers should dress accordingly. Summer is often the wettest season; however, rain may fall at any time. Waterproof clothing and footwear are vital for hikers to keep comfortable in changeable conditions.

- Hiking in hilly areas, such as the Bavarian Alps, necessitates awareness of altitude effects. Temperatures might drop dramatically as you climb height, and weather conditions can change quickly. Hikers should dress in layers to adjust to temperature changes and be mindful of the possibility of altitude-related difficulties.

- Daylight hours vary by season, with longer days in the summer and shorter days in the winter. Hikers should organize their pathways and activities properly, ensuring that they have enough daylight to complete their treks.

Hikers may make the most of their experience in Germany's gorgeous landscapes by understanding seasonal differences and being prepared for a variety of weather situations. The country's varied climate provides a hiking trip for any season, whether relishing in the warmth of summer or embracing the peacefulness of a winter trek.

Safety Tips and Regulations

Hiking in Germany is a great experience, but trail safety is critical. Following trail etiquette and being informed of emergency contacts and services help to ensure a safe and happy hiking journey.

Trail Etiquettes
Hiking trail etiquette is critical for protecting the natural environment, guaranteeing hiker safety, and encouraging a great trail experience for all:

- **Stay on Marked Trails:** Leaving marked trails may disrupt animal habitats and ecosystems. To reduce environmental effects, stick to approved pathways.

- Pack out everything garbage, including food wrappers and rubbish, and leave no trace. To preserve the natural beauty of your surroundings, follow the "Leave No Trace" guidelines.

- **Respect Wildlife:** Keep a safe distance from wildlife and avoid feeding them. Wildlife interactions are a natural part of the hiking experience, and keeping a respectful distance promotes the safety of both humans and wildlife.

- **Yield to Others:** Generally, uphill walkers have the right of way. Yield to other path users, whether they be hikers, bicyclists, or horseback riders. This helps to keep traffic flowing smoothly and reduces accidents.

- **Keep Noise Levels Low:** Embrace nature's serenity by limiting noise levels to a minimum. This enables other hikers to enjoy the sounds of the outdoors while also reducing animal disruptions.

- **Follow Local rules:** Be informed of and abide by unique hiking rules in each location. To conserve the ecology, certain trails may prohibit camping, off-leash dogs, or other activities.

- **Weather Awareness:** Be aware of shifting weather patterns. Check weather predictions before venturing out, and bring suitable clothes and equipment in case of unexpected weather changes.

Services and Emergency Contacts

While Germany has well-maintained hiking routes and an effective emergency response system, hikers should be prepared for the unexpected. Here are some crucial points to consider:

- **Emergency Numbers:** In Germany, the emergency number is 112. This number links you to the fire department, medical help, and other emergency services. Furthermore, each region may have its mountain rescue service for more distant places.

- **Inform Someone:** Inform a friend, family member, or the lodging where you will be staying of your trekking intentions. Share information like your route estimated return time, and emergency contact information.

- Carry a GPS gadget or a smartphone with GPS capability. Download offline maps of the hiking region to help you navigate if your network is down.

- Pack a basic first aid pack with necessities such as bandages, antiseptic wipes, pain relievers, and any personal prescriptions. Prepare to offer basic first aid while you wait for expert assistance.

- Consider packing a lightweight emergency shelter or space blanket, particularly if you're going on a longer or more distant trek. It offers critical protection in the event of unforeseen weather changes or calamities.

- **Know Your Limits:** Be honest with yourself about your hiking ability and physical condition. Avoid paths that are above your ability level, particularly in inclement weather.

- **Local Information Centers:** Learn about the information centers and ranger stations located along your path. They may provide help, information about trail conditions, and contact information for local emergency agencies.

- Consider purchasing travel insurance that covers hiking-related emergencies, including medical evacuation if necessary.

Hikers may go on their adventure with confidence, knowing they are well-prepared for a safe and pleasurable experience in Germany's stunning landscapes, by following trail etiquettes and remaining informed on emergency contacts and services.

TOP HIKING LOCATIONS

The Bavarian Alps

The Bavarian Alps are a magnificent tribute to Germany's alpine splendor, beckoning hikers to discover a world of towering peaks, clean lakes, and green meadows. This area, located in the country's south, has a multitude of trekking possibilities for hikers of all abilities.

Key Trails and Routes:

The Zugspitze Summit Trail is one of the most recognizable routes in the Bavarian Alps. This difficult path leads hikers to the top of the Zugspitze, Germany's highest mountain, where they may enjoy panoramic views of the surrounding alpine scenery. The rise rewards hikers with breathtaking views, while the descent enables them to marvel at the different flora and geological characteristics.

The Partnachklamm Gorge Trail is a beautiful choice for those looking for a less demanding trip. The Partnachklamm, a canyon created by the Partnach River, provides the setting for this trek. Hikers are guided down the small valley by wooden walkways, delivering a thrilling encounter among towering cliffs and gushing waterfalls.

The Eibsee Circular Trail, which circles the crystal-clear Eibsee Lake at the foot of the Zugspitze, is family-friendly. The walk provides stunning views of the surrounding mountains and is appropriate for hikers of all ages.

Noteworthy Landmarks and Natural Features:

Several locations in the Bavarian Alps provide cultural and historical dimension to the hiking experience. Perched atop a hill, the Neuschwanstein Castle is an architectural masterpiece right out of a fairy tale. Hikers may enjoy breathtaking views of the castle from a variety of routes in the area.

The Eibsee Cable Car is a marvel of engineering that lifts passengers to the peak of Zugspitze, providing a unique view of the alpine environment. The cable car ride is an experience in and of itself, with stunning panoramic vistas.

The natural characteristics of the Bavarian Alps are nothing short of breathtaking. The Wimbachklamm Gorge is a tiny gorge with flowing waterfalls that creates a dramatic and scenic scene. Hikers may walk through the canyon on wooden bridges and trails, surrounded by the peaceful sounds of water echoing off the rocks.

Another hidden beauty is the Alpsee Lake in the Alps' foothills. It provides a tranquil location for a leisurely trek, surrounded by deep woods and with the Alps as a background. The peaceful environment and the reflected waters make it a favorite among nature aficionados.

Every route in the Bavarian Alps leads to a discovery, whether it's a quaint alpine lodge, a secret stream, or a spectacular perspective. The mix of difficult walks and culturally important sites makes this location a must-see for hikers.

The Black Forest

The Black Forest, also known as the Schwarzwald in German, is a magical and enthralling terrain that has inspired mythology and fairy tales. Hiking across this huge wooded area is an absorbing experience, with each route unfolding a narrative of distinct vegetation, diversified animals, and breathtaking scenery.

Flora & Fauna:

The Black Forest is famous for its thick and old forests, which provide an ecology that supports a diverse range of flora and wildlife. Wildflowers litter the woodland floor, including the renowned cuckoo flower and the rare lady's slipper orchid. The lovely aroma of flowering flowers fills the air in spring, offering a sensory feast for trekkers.

A variety of fauna, including deer, foxes, and wild boars, may be found in the woodland. Birdwatchers will enjoy seeing species such as woodpeckers, owls, and the elusive capercaillie. Hikers may observe the natural cycle of the forest, from its waking in spring to its serenity in winter, thanks to the linked network of paths.

Scenic Viewpoints:

The Black Forest is a refuge for nature enthusiasts as well as those seeking panoramic vistas and beautiful outlooks. The Feldberg Summit Trail carries hikers to Feldberg Mountain, the highest point in the Black Forest. The expansive panoramas of lush woods, undulating hills, and distant settlements may be seen from the peak.

The Mummelsee Loop Trail surrounds the Mummelsee, the Black Forest's biggest and deepest cirque lake. Hikers are rewarded with breathtaking views of the lake, which is bordered by pine trees. The serene environment is created by the quietness of the lake and the surrounding tranquility.

The Hornisgrinde Circular Trail leads hikers to the Hornisgrinde, a plateau with expansive panoramas, for a more dramatic outlook. On clear days, the Alps may be seen in the distance, offering a stunning contrast to the Black Forest's dark, lush vastness.

Although not a standard hiking path, the Triberg Waterfalls are a must-see natural sight. The waterfalls drop down a series of stairs surrounded by thick flora, providing a stunning scene. Hikers may enjoy the pleasant mist and the calming sounds of gushing water by exploring the routes surrounding the falls.

Every route in the Black Forest provides a unique combination of natural beauty and cultural riches. Hikers may immerse themselves in the beauty of this fabled forest, from the rich flora and wildlife to the sweeping perspectives, generating memories that remain like the whispers of old trees.

Saxon Switzerland National Park

Rock Formations and Difficult Trails:

The Saxon Switzerland National Park, located in the Elbe Sandstone Mountains, is a natural paradise filled with breathtaking rock formations, steep valleys, and lush woods. Hiking in this national park reveals a landscape formed by millennia of natural processes.

The Bastei Bridge Trail is a well-known trail that leads hikers to the famed Bastei Bridge, which crosses a stunning sandstone rock structure. The Elbe River snakes through the sandstone cliffs and the huge expanse of the national park below may be seen from this vantage point.

The Schrammsteine Loop is a fantastic experience for those looking for more difficult courses. This trail leads hikers through tight fissures and steep ascents, with panoramic views of the harsh sandstone cliffs. The Elbe Sandstone Mountains, with their different peaks and towers, provide an exciting playground for both rock climbers and hikers.

Hiking the Affenstein Promenade immerses hikers in a maze of towering rock formations, each with its distinct personality. The rocky terrain and interplay of light and shadow create an otherworldly ambiance, making it popular among photographers and nature lovers.

Safety Precautions in the Park:

While the trails in Saxon Switzerland National Park provide an exciting adventure, the following safety measures are essential for a pleasant experience:

- **Footwear:** The paths may be difficult, with uneven terrain and steep ascents. Stability requires the use of strong hiking footwear with high traction.

- **Weather Awareness:** The weather in the park may change quickly. Hikers should check the weather forecast before starting and be prepared for rapid temperature fluctuations. Rain may make paths treacherous, so use additional care.

- **Trail Signs:** The park is crisscrossed by a network of pathways, making it easy to get lost. To prevent being confused, pay close attention to path markers and signs, particularly in the labyrinthine rock formations.

- **Rock Climbing Safety:** Before embarking on rock climbing activities, be sure you have the essential equipment and expertise. Be careful of your limitations as well as the difficulty level of the climbing routes.

- **Respect for fauna:** Saxon Switzerland is home to a varied range of fauna. While interactions with animals are uncommon, it is crucial to keep a respectful distance from them. To reduce the effect, do not feed wildlife and dispose of any garbage.

- **Emergency Contacts:** Learn who to call in an emergency and where to find ranger stations throughout the park.

Knowing how to seek assistance in an emergency is critical.

The beautiful landscapes of Saxon Switzerland National Park entice hikers to explore its distinctive rock formations and engage in demanding expeditions. Visitors may completely enjoy the natural beauty while also assuring a safe and pleasant trip by following safety procedures.

Harz National Park

Ecosystem Diversity:

Harz National Park in central Germany is a refuge for nature lovers, with a patchwork of varied ecosystems. The park's landscapes, which range from deep woods to high plateaus, are influenced by a complex geological and ecological history.

The Brocken Loop Trail leads hikers to the top of the Brocken, the Harz Mountains' highest mountain. The walk winds through gorgeous spruce woods, affording sightings of local species along the way. Hikers are rewarded with magnificent views of the Harz region's various terrain at the peak.

The Ilsetal Valley Trail follows the course of the Ilse River through a verdant valley. Hikers are surrounded by lush trees, and the calming sound of the running river adds to the peacefulness of the trip. The valley is home to many plant species, resulting in a botanical paradise.

The Teufelsmauer (Devil's Wall) Trail brings hikers to a stunning sandstone structure resembling a huge wall for those interested in distinctive geological characteristics. This natural marvel bears witness to the geological processes that produced the Harz terrain.

Trailside Historical Attractions:

Harz National Park is not simply a natural haven, but also a historically significant territory. Hikers discover historical sites along the hiking paths, which offer a cultural component to their adventure.

The Harz Witches' Trail links various places related to witch trials and folklore in the area. Hikers may learn about the cultural relevance of these legends by visiting places like the Brocken, where witches were thought to congregate.

The Goslar Mines Trail takes visitors on a fascinating tour of the Rammelsberg Mines, a UNESCO World Heritage site. Hikers may learn about the region's mining history and tour restored mining sites to get insight into Harz's industrial past.

The St. Andreasberg Mining Trail offers an insight into the Harz Mountains' mining history. Hikers may visit historic mining sites, see the remains of mining buildings, and learn about the difficulties that miners encountered centuries ago.

Harz National Park combines natural beauty and historical legacies to provide an unforgettable hiking experience. Hikers become part of the fabric that distinguishes the Harz Mountains as they cross varied habitats and uncover evidence of the region's rich history.

TRAIL SELECTION AND DIFFICULTY LEVELS

Overview of Trail Difficulty Ratings

Hiking needs a detailed awareness of trail difficulty ratings to help hikers pick routes that match their ability levels and interests. In

Germany, trail difficulty is often divided into three categories:

Easy/Beginner Trails:

These routes are ideal for beginners and families, with gradual slopes, well-maintained pathways, and little elevation increase. The terrain is relatively flat, making it suited for people of all fitness levels. Beginner paths are a wonderful beginning to hiking, enabling newbies to appreciate nature without encountering too many difficult hurdles.

Moderate/Intermediate Trails:

Intermediate paths provide a moderate degree of difficulty for hikers with some experience and a fair level of fitness. Steeper inclines, uneven terrain, and longer lengths may be encountered on these paths. Intermediate paths increase in complexity, enabling hikers to put their endurance and abilities to the test while still providing a reasonable experience for those looking for a little more adventure.

Difficult/Advanced Trails:

Advanced paths are designed for experienced hikers looking for a more tough experience. These paths often have steep climbs, rough terrain, and lengthy lengths. Hikers heading into advanced trails should be fit, agile, and have solid navigation abilities. These routes provide a gratifying experience for individuals who want to test their boundaries and explore more difficult terrain.

Specialized/Technical Trails:

Some paths, such as rock-climbing routes, via Ferratas, and alpine trails, may fall into specific categories. These need particular skills and equipment, such as climbing gear and technical expertise. Specialized trails provide a one-of-a-kind and exciting experience for individuals with the necessary skills.

Understanding these difficulty classifications enables hikers to make educated decisions, ensuring that the paths they choose are appropriate for their fitness levels and experience. It is critical to honestly evaluate individual skills and progressively go from easy to more difficult terrain as confidence and experience improve.

Family-Friendly Trails

Germany is a great hiking destination for families, with a variety of paths to suit all ages and abilities. Family-friendly paths promote safety, accessibility, and kid-friendly elements. Here are some great family-friendly hikes:

Eibsee Circular Trail (Bavarian Alps):

For families, a short circle around the scenic Eibsee Lake at the foot of the Zugspitze is excellent. The level terrain, gorgeous lake views, and picnic options make it an ideal visit for both youngsters and parents.

Hexenstieg Trail (Harz National Park):

The Hexenstieg, or Witches' Trail, has portions that are ideal for children. Families may study the region's mythology and enjoy the mild slopes and well-marked routes while hiking through the magnificent Harz scenery.

Schwarzatal Panorama Trail (Thuringian Forest):

This hike combines family-friendly features with breathtaking vistas. The trail's relatively level slope and interpretative signage make it instructive and fun for youngsters. The path travels through gorgeous scenery and allows for nature exploration.

Pfälzer Weinsteig (Palatinate Forest):
In the Palatinate Forest, the Pfälzer Weinsteig has family-friendly parts. This route combines woodland pathways, meadows, and picturesque towns to create a diverse and engaging experience for families.

Interactive components such as informative signage, playgrounds, and easy-to-follow routes are common on family-friendly trails. These paths seek to develop in youngsters a love of nature while also offering a relaxing and delightful experience for the whole family.

Advanced and Challenging Routes for Experienced Hikers

Germany has a multitude of difficult routes that cross rough terrains, climb towering summits, and present challenges that test physical and mental stamina for seasoned hikers looking for more rigorous and demanding excursions. Here are some examples of advanced routes:

Watzmann Traverse (Bavarian Alps):

The Watzmann Traverse is a difficult climb that takes hikers over the famous Watzmann Massif. This strenuous terrain includes steep ascents and exposed portions, and it requires a high degree of fitness and mountain knowledge.

Rennsteig Trail (Thuringian Forest and Harz):

The Rennsteig is a long-distance path with varied topography, including difficult stretches through the Thuringian Forest and the Harz Mountains. Parts of this path may be tackled by experienced hikers, going through deep woods and scaling the highest summits.

Königstour der Alpen (Allgäu Alps):

The Königstour, or King's Tour, is a challenging path in the Allgäu Alps that covers alpine scenery, high slopes, and rocky terrain. This difficult trail rewards hikers with stunning vistas, but it needs technical skill and stamina.

Elbe Sandstone Mountains High Route (Saxon Switzerland National Park):

The High Route in the Elbe Sandstone Mountains provides an advanced experience for hikers looking for a challenge among distinctive rock formations. This track, which winds through difficult terrain and rock formations, requires both physical strength and rock-climbing ability.

Advanced routes may include substantial elevation gain, and exposed parts, and require the use of specialist equipment such as trekking poles and, in some circumstances, climbing gear. Hikers must be well-prepared, physically fit, and knowledgeable to tackle these difficult routes.

Multi-Day Hikes and Long-Distance Trails

Multi-day walks and long-distance paths provide an immersive experience for individuals who like lengthy hiking experiences and want to see Germany's different landscapes. These pathways enable hikers to immerse themselves in the country's natural beauty and cultural riches:

Eifelsteig (Eifel Mountains):
The Eifelsteig is a long-distance route that winds across the Eifel Mountains, taking in woods, meadows, and historical places. Hikers may opt to hike chunks or the full path, taking in the various scenery and attractive communities.

Rheinsteig (Rhine Valley):

The Rheinsteig is a long-distance route that follows the Rhine River and offers hikers magnificent vistas of vineyards, castles, and the river itself. The track traverses a variety of terrains, from difficult accents to pleasant riverfront pathways.

Harzer-Hexen-Stieg (Harz Mountains):

The Harzer-Hexen-Stieg, often known as the Harz Witches' Trail, is a multi-day trip through the magical sceneries of the Harz Mountains. It provides a whole Harz experience, with different scenery, historical attractions, and attractive lodgings along the route.

Altmühltal Panorama Trail (Bavaria):

The Altmühltal Panorama Trail travels through the Altmühltal Nature Park, providing hikers with a multi-day excursion that includes different landscapes, river vistas, and ancient site visits. The route allows for cultural inquiry as well as interactions with local flora and animals.

Multi-day walks and long-distance routes need meticulous preparation, including accommodations, food, and route navigation. Hikers should be prepared for various terrain and shifting weather conditions to have a fascinating and engaging adventure across the landscapes of Germany.

EQUIPMENT AND GEAR

Essential gear for hiking in Germany

Hiking in Germany, with its varied landscapes and fluctuating weather conditions, requires careful planning of necessary equipment to provide a safe and pleasurable trip. Here's a thorough list of the equipment that every hiker should have:

Walking Boots:

Purchase durable, comfortable hiking footwear with enough ankle support. The terrain in Germany may be challenging, and decent boots give stability and protection against uneven ground.

Clothing for the Weather:

Layer your clothing to adjust to shifting weather conditions. It is critical to have a moisture-wicking base layer, an insulating mid-layer, and a waterproof and windproof upper layer. Consider investing in a breathable rain jacket to keep you dry during unexpected rain storms.

Hat for Bad Weather:

A brimmed hat shields you from the heat in the summer, while a waterproof hat keeps you dry when it rains. A thick beanie helps maintain heat in chilly weather.

Backpack:

To carry your necessities, choose a comfortable and adequately sized backpack. Padded shoulder straps, a hip belt for weight distribution, and various pockets for organized storage are all desirable characteristics.

Navigation Tools:

Bring a thorough map of your trekking route as well as a dependable compass. While GPS gadgets and smartphone applications with offline maps are useful, having classic navigation tools as backups is critical.

Hydration System:

Bring a water bottle or hydration kit to remain hydrated, particularly during the hotter months. Although some paths may have water sources, it is best to bring extra water for the whole journey.

Food and Snacks:

Bring energy-boosting foods such as trail mix, energy bars, and fruits with you. Bring a packed lunch for longer walks. If you want to eat along the way, get acquainted with the local cuisine.

First Aid Supplies:

Make a small first aid kit containing bandages, antiseptic wipes, pain relievers, and any personal prescriptions. Include insect repellant and blister pads.

Knife or Multitool:

A multi-tool or a solid knife may come in handy for a variety of scenarios, from cutting meals to dealing with unforeseen trail problems.

Headlamp or Flashlight:

Carry a dependable torch or headlamp with extra batteries, particularly if you want to trek early in the morning or late in the evening.

Emergency Shelter:

In the event of unforeseen weather changes or crises, a lightweight emergency shelter or space blanket offers protection. It's a little but useful addition to your arsenal.

Personal Identification and Emergency Contacts:

In your bag, have a copy of your identity, insurance information, and emergency contacts. It's critical in case of an emergency.

Clothing Considerations Based on the Season

Understanding seasonal differences in Germany is critical for choosing proper apparel. Here's a summary of what to wear in each season:

Spring (March to May):
- To adjust to changing temperatures, dress in breathable layers.

- For spring rains, a waterproof jacket is important.
- Consider convertible pants that can be worn as shorts as the weather warms up.

Summer months (June to August):
- Staying cool requires wearing lightweight, breathable clothes.
- Sun protection is provided with a wide-brimmed hat and sunglasses.
- Warm weather calls for hiking shorts and moisture-wicking tops.

Autumn (September to November):
- Layer your clothing for cold mornings and warmer afternoons.
- Autumn rains need the use of a waterproof and windproof garment.
- For chilly weather, consider wearing long pants and a light fleece.

Winter (December to February):

- Snow and low weather necessitate the use of insulated and waterproof footwear.

- Layer with thermal underwear, a fleece or down jacket, and a waterproof outer layer.

- To keep warm, put on a thick hat, gloves, and insulated socks.

Recommended Backpack Contents

A well-packed backpack improves comfort and outdoor readiness. Here is a thorough breakdown of suggested content:

Communication and Navigation:

- Compass and map.

- Offline maps on a GPS gadget or smartphone.
- Emergency siren.

Nutrition and Hydration:
- Hydration system or water bottle.
- Snacks and a packed lunch are provided.
- On longer walks, bring light cookware for hot drinks or meals.

Footwear and Clothing:
- Dress appropriately for the weather (as described above).
- Extra socks and apparel are recommended in case of unexpected weather changes.

First Aid and Safety:
- First-aid supplies.
- Knife or multitool.

- With extra batteries, use a flashlight or headlamp.

Comfort and Shelter:
- A space blanket or an emergency shelter.
- Sitting pad that is lightweight and small.
- Insect repellant for the warmer months.

Personal Effects:
- Personal identity, insurance details, and emergency contact information are all required.
- Lip balm and sunscreen.
- Items for personal hygiene, such as hand sanitizer and tissues.

Repairs Kit:
- Duct tape is useful for making rapid repairs.
- Sewing kit for gear repairs.

Extras:

- For capturing memories, use a camera or a smartphone.
- Binoculars are useful for birding or seeing picturesque vistas.
- Identification guide for flora and wildlife.

Specialized Equipment for Specific Trails

Due to their specific obstacles, many routes in Germany may need the use of specialist equipment. Here are some examples of specialist trail equipment:

Alpine Trails (e.g., Zugspitze Summit Trail):
- Mountaineering boots that can be used with crampons.

- For tricky portions, use a climbing harness and a helmet.
- For snow-covered terrain, use an ice axe.

Rock Climbing Trails (e.g., Elbe Sandstone Mountains High Route):
- Climbing boots with a solid foot positioning.
- A climbing helmet provides head protection.
- Chalk bag for climbing portions' hand grip.

Via Ferratas (e.g., Königstour der Alpen):
- Set of lanyards and a harness for a Via Ferrata.
- Climbing helmet to protect against falling debris.
- Gloves that help you hold the via Ferrata cables.

Winter Trails (e.g., Snowshoeing in the Bavarian Alps):

- Snow boots that are both insulated and waterproof.

- Snowshoes are used for walking in the snow.

- Warm apparel during the winter.

Adapting your gear to the trail's requirements offers a safer and more pleasurable hiking experience. Prioritize lightweight and compact solutions, and constantly consider the specific obstacles provided by the selected trail's terrain and weather conditions.

ACCOMMODATIONS AND SERVICES

Lodging Options Along Popular Hiking Routes

Germany has a wide variety of hotel alternatives along its famed hiking trails, appealing to a wide range of interests and budgets. Hikers may find adequate lodgings ranging from lovely guesthouses to mountain cabins to rest and refresh on their trips.

Many hiking trails are lined with guesthouses, inns, and bed-and-breakfast places. These lodgings are more comfortable and generally more customized. They are often family-run establishments that provide a welcoming ambiance and the opportunity to engage with locals. Some guest houses also provide traditional regional meals, enabling hikers to experience the tastes of the area.

Alpine huts, which are particularly common in hilly places such as the Bavarian Alps, provide a rustic but immersive accommodation experience. These mountain cottages often provide modest facilities like bunk beds and common eating spaces. Hikers may wake up to spectacular mountain views and interact with other outdoor enthusiasts by staying in an alpine hut.

Hotels and resorts are available in and around renowned hiking sites for those looking for a more upscale experience. These institutions provide a variety of amenities, including spa services, exquisite dining selections, and comfortable accommodations. Many hotels also provide shuttle services or guided trips to hikers interested in exploring the local surroundings.

In addition, some long-distance paths have designated lodging along the way. Pilgrim routes, like the Camino de Santiago, provide pilgrim hostels known as "refugios" where hikers may find modest accommodation, encouraging fellowship among other pilgrims.

Hikers may select between a quiet guesthouse in a picturesque town, an alpine cabin for an authentic mountain experience, or a hotel for a touch of luxury after a day on the trails.

Camping Facilities and Regulations

Camping is a popular alternative for hikers looking for a deeper connection to nature and a more affordable lodging option. Camping facilities and rules vary by location in Germany, and following the requirements is critical for a safe and happy camping experience.

Campgrounds:

There are established campsites all around Germany, particularly in rural and natural locations. These amenities include restrooms, showers, and grilling places, as well as specific tent spots. For individuals who prefer a more enclosed environment, several campsites provide cottages or bungalows.

Camping in the wild:

While wild camping is normally prohibited in many areas, there are certain exceptions. limited regions, such as the Harz Mountains, allow wild camping with limited limits. To maintain appropriate camping habits, it is important to study and follow local legislation.

Long-Distance Hikes:

Some long-distance paths have designated camping spots along the way. Hikers on paths such as the Westweg in the Black Forest or the Eifelsteig may come across authorized camping areas with minimal amenities such as water sources and trash disposal facilities.

Leave No Trace:

Regardless of the camping choice selected, hikers should follow the "Leave No Trace" guidelines, which include packing out all garbage, respecting animals and plants, and limiting environmental damage.

Restrictions and Permissions:

In areas where wild camping is legal, it is essential to get the necessary licenses and abide by any limitations. Some regions may have limits at particular periods of the year or for special purposes of environmental protection.

Camping offers a unique chance to immerse oneself in Germany's natural surroundings. Hikers should plan and choose camping alternatives with caution, ensuring that their selections are by local legislation and conservation initiatives.

Local Services and Amenities in Hiking Areas

Hiking locations in Germany are well-equipped with the necessary services and facilities to meet hikers' demands. These local services improve the hiking experience by offering convenience and help along the way.

Cafés and Restaurants:
Hikers may discover a range of eateries and cafés providing local and foreign food along popular hiking trails, particularly in tourist sites.

These places allow you to recharge with a big meal or take a calm break with a cup of coffee.

Grocery Stores and Markets:

In surrounding villages or towns, many hiking destinations feature food shops or marketplaces. Before hitting the trails, hikers may load up on necessities, snacks, and fresh food. This is especially helpful for individuals who are planning multi-day treks or camping vacations.

Outdoor Equipment Stores:

Hiking locations often contain outdoor equipment stores where hikers may buy or rent equipment and gear. These stores may sell anything from apparel and footwear to camping gear and accessories.

Medical Services:

Medical facilities, pharmacies, and first aid services are usually available in villages and towns surrounding hiking areas. Hikers should know where these facilities are in case of an emergency and carry a basic first aid kit.

Accommodations:

Hiking destinations may contain mountain huts, shelters, or cottages particularly constructed for hikers, in addition to the hotel alternatives described above. These amenities provide a spot to relax, have a hot meal, and socialize with other hikers.

Tourist Information Offices:

Tourist information centers in hiking locations provide useful resources such as maps, route information, and local knowledge. Hikers may stop by these facilities to get important information on the trails, weather, and current warnings.

Transportation Services:

Many hiking trails are accessible by public transit. Hikers may make use of easy transit choices such as train stations and bus stops near trailheads, allowing for more flexible route planning.

The provision of these services means that hikers have access to essential resources and assistance, making hiking in Germany more fun and comfortable.

Transportation Options to and Within Hiking Destinations

Hiking sites in Germany are easily accessible because of a well-developed transportation system, which provides hikers with a variety of alternatives for reaching trailheads and navigating the country.

Public Transportation:

Germany has a well-developed and efficient public transportation system. Trains and buses link large cities to hiking areas, allowing hikers to access trailheads without the need for a private car. Public transportation is eco-friendly and provides picturesque access to many hiking spots.

Regional Buses and Trains:

Regional rail services, such as the Bayerische Regiobahn in Bavaria and the Harz-Elbe-Express in the Harz Mountains, link smaller cities and villages to hiking regions. Buses supplement train services by reaching more isolated trailheads and providing more route flexibility.

Ride Sharing and Car Rentals:

Car rentals are accessible at major towns and airports for hikers who want flexibility and freedom. Car-sharing services are particularly useful for individuals who want to visit more rural or less accessible hiking spots.

Shuttle Transportation:

Shuttle services for hikers are available in several areas, offering transportation to and from trailheads. These services are especially widespread in popular hiking areas where public transportation may be restricted.

Local Taxis:

Local taxi services may be an alternative for transportation to and from trailheads in rural locations and smaller cities. It is best to confirm availability and plan ahead of time, particularly in less populous areas.

Trailhead Parking:

Many trailheads include parking for hikers who have their automobiles. It is important to check for any parking laws or fees and to park cars in specific zones.

Biking and Cycling:

Hikers in certain areas may explore routes by bicycle or e-bike. Cycling lanes and bike rentals may be provided, offering an eco-friendly and active means of transportation.

A mix of different modes of transportation makes it possible to navigate inside hiking locations. Hikers may pick the form of transportation that best meets their tastes and trail access needs, whether they use public transit, hire a vehicle, or use specialist services.

CULTURAL AND CULINARY ADVENTURES

Cultural Attractions Along the Trails

Hiking in Germany combines natural beauties with a rich tapestry of cultural elements along the paths. Hikers may immerse themselves in Germany's cultural history as they explore the different landscapes, from historic sites to medieval communities.

Fortresses and castles:

Many of Germany's castles and fortifications are conveniently positioned along hiking trails. The Rhine Valley, for example, is home to the renowned Lorelei Rock as well as other castles located on the slopes, which provide a touch of medieval history to the hiking experience.

Religious Sites and Pilgrim Routes:

Pilgrim paths like the Camino de Santiago allow walkers to explore medieval cathedrals, chapels, and monasteries. These places provide insights into Germany's religious past and often include one-of-a-kind architectural and artistic components.

Historical Towns and Villages:

Hiking paths often pass through picturesque old towns and villages. Rothenburg ob der Tauber on the Romantic Road and Quedlinburg in the Harz Mountains are examples of well-preserved medieval villages with cobblestone lanes and half-timbered buildings that transport hikers back in time.

Cultural Environments:

Some pathways go through cultural landscapes that have been altered by millennia of human activity. The Moselle River, which is flanked by vineyards and attractive towns, shows the region's cultural importance in wine production. These landscapes depict human connection with the environment.

Sculptures and Art Installations:

Art installations and sculptures are often seen on modern hiking paths, bringing a contemporary cultural component to the outdoor experience. The Eifel Kunst-Wanderweg, for example, incorporates art into the natural environment, resulting in a participatory adventure for hikers.

Hikers in Germany may experience not only the natural beauty of the country but also the cultural legacy that creates the character of various areas. The pathways' blending of history, art, and architecture gives a complete and rewarding hiking experience.

Local Festivals and Events

Germany's calendar is jam-packed with festivals and events that highlight the country's rich cultural variety. Hikers may time their trips to coincide with these celebrations, which will lend a bright and festive ambiance to their outdoor travels.

Oktoberfest (Munich):
Oktoberfest is one of the world's most renowned beer festivals, held each year in Munich. While it may not coincide with hiking

seasons exactly, hikers going through Bavaria in late September may enjoy the vibrant environment, traditional music, and, of course, a range of German beers.

Christmas Markets (Various Cities):

Christmas markets convert cities and towns into festive wonderlands throughout the winter season. Hikers exploring routes near towns like Nuremberg, Dresden, and Cologne may take in the magnificent ambiance, festive decorations, and traditional Christmas foods.

Wine Festivals (Rhine and Moselle Valleys):

The Rhine and Moselle Valleys are well known for their vineyards and winemaking. Hikers in these areas may attend local wine festivals to taste regional wines, learn about wine-making traditions, and enjoy live music and celebrations.

Harvest Festivals (Various Regions):

Harvest festivals are held in many places around Germany, highlighting local products, traditional crafts, and folk music. Hikers traveling through agricultural settings, such as the Palatinate region, may come upon these events, which provide a flavor of rural customs.

Folk and Music Festivals (Various Regions):

Throughout the year, Germany holds several folk and music events. Hikers might come upon these events, which include traditional dances, music performances, and cultural displays, in both urban and rural locations.

Hikers may not only appreciate Germany's natural beauty but also connect with its active cultural scene by coordinating their hiking plans with local festivals and events, generating unique experiences that extend beyond the trails.

Traditional German Cuisine for Hikers

German food is robust and savory, making it ideal for hikers looking for healthy meals to fuel their excursions. Traditional foods provide a taste of regional delicacies while hiking paths provide a gastronomic voyage.

Pretzels and Sausages:

Hikers must try classic German sausages such as Bratwurst or Currywurst. Combine them with a soft pretzel for a traditional and enjoyable trailside supper. These classic sweets are often available from street sellers and local markets.

Obatzda and Bavarian Pretzels:

Hikers in Bavaria may eat giant Bavarian pretzels with Obatzda, a delectable cheese spread prepared with Camembert, butter, and spices. This combo makes a tasty and invigorating snack.

Sauerbraten:

Hikers may eat sauerbraten, a pot roast marinated in a sour-sweet sauce, in a variety of places. This slow-cooked pork, which is often served with red cabbage and dumplings, delivers a filling and energy-dense dinner.

Kartoffelsalat (Potato Salad) and Wurst:

Kartoffelsalat, or potato salad, is a popular dish in Germany. Hikers may match it with locally produced Wurst (sausage) for a full and portable supper. This combo is prevalent in local restaurants and events.

Käsespätzle:

Käsespätzle, or macaroni and cheese in German, is a cozy meal prepared with egg noodles, melted cheese, and caramelized onions. Käsespätzle may be found at traditional pubs and mountain cabins by hikers looking for a warm and pleasant supper.

Red Grütze:

Rote Grütze, a sweet dessert created with red berries and served with vanilla sauce, is a light way to conclude a trek. This dish makes use of the profusion of berries available throughout the summer months.

Recommended Places to Try Local Dishes

Beer Gardens in Munich:

Munich's beer gardens provide an authentic backdrop for traditional Bavarian fare. Hikers may enjoy regional delicacies with freshly brewed beer while taking in the vibrant ambiance of these legendary restaurants.

Vineyard Restaurants in Rhine and Moselle Valleys:

Hikers may discover vineyard eateries that offer local wines coupled with regional foods along the trails in the Rhine and Moselle Valleys. These restaurants provide panoramic views of the vineyards and the river, making for an unforgettable dining experience.

Historic Inns along Romantic Road:

The Romantic Road is noted for its scenic towns and old inns that serve regional cuisine. Hikers may enjoy the beauty of these inns while dining on traditional German fare.

Local Taverns in the Black Forest:

The Black Forest, with its deep woodlands and lovely towns, is home to medieval taverns. Hikers may eat Black Forest ham, smoked sausages, and other delights at these quaint eateries.

Street Food Markets in Berlin:

Berlin's lively street food markets, such as Markthalle Neun, provide a wide range of gastronomic delicacies. In a vibrant market environment, hikers touring the city may enjoy a range of German and foreign foods.

Hikers may refill their energies while enjoying savoring the distinctive tastes of Germany's culinary heritage by exploring local cafes and markets along their hiking paths. Hikers will have a great culinary adventure at these suggested locations, which range from street food booths to historic inns.

ENVIRONMENTAL CONSERVATION

Principles of Leave No Trace

Hiking in Germany, like hiking anywhere else, imposes a duty on outdoor lovers to reduce their environmental effects. The concepts of Leave No Trace give a foundation for ethical and sustainable outdoor enjoyment. Here is a summary of these concepts and their application to hiking in Germany:

Plan and Prepare:

Before going on a trek, plan your route, check the weather, and be aware of local rules. Adequate planning decreases the chance of an emergency and equips you for appropriate outdoor leisure.

Travel and Camp on Durable Surfaces:

To minimize the damage to plants and soil, stick to designated pathways and campsites. Well-maintained trails in Germany are intended to direct walkers through picturesque places while maintaining the underlying ecosystems.

Proper Waste Disposal:

Remove all trash, including litter and food remnants. Hikers should be vigilant in disposing of rubbish in appropriate containers and following local recycling standards since Germany puts a significant focus on waste separation and recycling.

Leave What You Find:

Leave rocks, trees, and historical objects in their original state to preserve the natural environment. This philosophy assures that future hikers will be able to experience the same natural and cultural aspects.

Minimize Campfire Impact:

Use designated fire rings and keep flames modest if campfires are allowed. Because open fires may be prohibited in certain areas of Germany owing to environmental concerns, it is important to follow local restrictions.

Respect Wildlife:

Keep a safe distance between yourself and animals to prevent upsetting their natural habits.

Hikers should emphasize the maintenance of local ecosystems since Germany is home to varied flora and animals.

Be Mindful of Other Visitors:
Respect your fellow hikers' enjoyment of the outdoors and keep noise levels to a minimum. German trials often draw both locals and foreign tourists, and a courteous demeanor improves everyone's experience.

Hikers who follow the Leave No Trace principles help to the protection of Germany's natural beauty while enjoying the outdoors responsibly.

Conservation Initiatives in Hiking Areas

Germany has undertaken several conservation programs aimed at protecting its natural landscapes and promoting sustainable outdoor enjoyment. These efforts include cooperation among environmental groups, government agencies, and local people to safeguard the country's biodiversity and maintain natural balance in hiking areas.

National and Regional Parks:

National parks in Germany, such as the Bavarian Forest National Park and the Jasmund National Park, play an important role in conservation efforts. These protected areas provide habitat for a variety of plant and animal species, and tight laws are in place to limit human damage.

Trail Maintenance and Restoration:

Trail maintenance and restoration operations are often included in conservation programs. Maintaining well-defined trails reduces the effect on vulnerable ecosystems by preventing the formation of illegal routes. Restoration activities are focused on repairing places that have suffered deterioration.

Biodiversity Conservation Programs:

Many German areas have plans in place to maintain and increase biodiversity. These activities may involve reforestation operations, habitat restoration, and endangered species monitoring. Hikers may come across educational signs along trails emphasizing the significance of biodiversity protection.

Waste Reduction Campaigns:

In hiking regions, initiatives encouraging garbage minimization and proper rubbish disposal are frequent. Hikers are encouraged to carry out all rubbish, recycle responsibly, and reduce their ecological imprint via signage and educational efforts.

Environmental Education Centers:

Near hiking areas, environmental education centers give information on local ecosystems, conservation strategies, and the necessity of preserving natural habitats. These facilities provide educational activities for schools, families, and hikers to increase environmental awareness.

Partnerships with Outdoor Organizations:

Collaborations between environmental groups, hiking clubs, and government agencies aid in conservation efforts. These collaborations might include combined activities for trail maintenance, animal conservation, and sustainable tourism practices.

Conservation efforts in hiking areas demonstrate Germany's dedication to protecting its natural heritage. Hikers may help by keeping on designated paths, following conservation principles, and being informed about local conservation projects.

Responsible Tourism Practices

Responsible tourism practices are critical for ensuring that hikers positively contribute to the environment and communities they visit. Responsible tourism in Germany is consistent with the country's commitment to sustainability and conservation. Hikers should follow the following guidelines:

Choosing Sustainable Accommodations:
Choose sustainable lodgings, such as eco-friendly hotels, guesthouses, or lodges.

Environmental standards and eco-certifications are followed by many businesses in Germany.

Taking Public Transportation:

To get to hiking regions, make use of Germany's effective public transit infrastructure. Individual travel decreases carbon emissions and has a lower environmental effect when taken by public transportation.

Helping Local Communities:

Choose to eat at local restaurants, shop at local markets, and interact with the communities you visit. Supporting local companies benefits the region's economic well-being.

Use Ethical Wildlife Viewing Techniques:

When approaching animals, keep a respectful distance and watch from a safe distance. Avoid feeding or disturbing animals, and follow any conservation recommendations that are presented.

Water and Energy Conservation:
Conserve water and energy at your lodgings and on the route. Take shorter showers, switch off lights when not in use, and use water properly to save resources.

Learn About the Local Culture:
Discover the cultural norms and customs of the places you visit. Respect for local traditions promotes healthy relationships and improves cross-cultural understanding.

Leave Cultural and Natural Features Untouched:
Touching or interfering with cultural objects, historical places, and natural features is strictly prohibited. Keep these places in good condition for future generations.

Contribute to Conservation Efforts:

Consider volunteering or donating to conservation efforts in the locations you visit. Many environmental groups appreciate the help of ethical tourists.

Hikers may help to ensure the sustainability of Germany's hiking destinations by practicing responsible tourism, reducing their environmental effects, and supporting the well-being of local communities.

ADDITIONAL RESOURCES AND INFORMATION

Hiking Maps

Germany, with its wide network of hiking routes, provides a wealth of tools to assist hikers in planning and navigating their excursions. Hiking maps and guidebooks are essential resources for people exploring the country's different landscapes.

- **Kompass Maps:** Kompass is a well-known producer of hiking maps for several places in Germany. These precise topographic maps include routes, altitudes, and sites of interest. They are accessible in various sizes, ranging from local pathways to long-distance trails.

- **Outdooractive Maps:** The Outdooractive platform provides precise maps for hiking, biking, and other outdoor activities. The interactive maps provide real-time data such as elevation profiles, trail conditions, and places of interest. Routes may be planned and maps downloaded for offline usage.

- **OpenStreetMap (OSM)** is a collaborative mapping project based on user-generated data. OSM is used as a foundation map by several hiking applications and websites, including Outdooractive. The benefit is that users may help improve the accuracy of trail data.

Online Forums and Communities for Hikers

Connecting with other hikers and gaining real-world experiences is a rewarding component of the hiking experience. Hikers in Germany may use online forums and groups to share information, seek assistance, and establish a feeling of community.

Outdooractive Community:
Website: Outdooractive Community
Description: Outdoor Active's community platform allows hikers to share their experiences, upload photos, and exchange insights on specific trails. Users can ask questions, provide recommendations, and connect with like-minded outdoor enthusiasts.

Wanderlust Forum:

Website: Wanderlust Forum

Description: Wanderlust, a travel magazine with a focus on outdoor activities, has an active forum where hikers can discuss their experiences in Germany. The forum covers a wide range of topics, including gear recommendations, trail suggestions, and travel tips.

Deutscher Alpenverein (German Alpine Club) Forum:

Website: DAV Forum

Description: The German Alpine Club's forum is a community hub for mountaineers, climbers, and hikers. Hikers can find discussions on alpine regions, trail conditions, and equipment. The forum is in German, reflecting the local focus.

Reddit – r/Germany and r/Hiking:

Subreddits: r/Germany and r/Hiking

Description: Reddit provides a global platform for discussions. The r/Germany subreddit is suitable for general travel inquiries, while r/Hiking is a space for discussing hiking experiences, seeking advice, and sharing photos. Both offer opportunities to connect with the hiking community.

Meetup:

Website: Meetup Hiking Groups in Germany

Description: Meetup is a platform for finding and building local communities. Hikers in Germany can join or create hiking groups to organize outings, share experiences, and meet new people who share a passion for the outdoors.

Facebook Groups:

Examples: "Hiking in Germany," "Germany Hiking and Outdoor Adventures," and regional-specific groups.

Description: Facebook groups are active communities where hikers share information about trails, ask for advice, and organize group hikes. These groups provide a social platform for connecting with other hikers.

Hikers may tap into a wealth of information, get insights from experienced folks, and develop a feeling of community with other outdoor lovers by participating in online forums and groups. These sites are useful for both organizing walks and connecting with others in the hiking community.

Tourist Information Centers

Tourist information centers play an important role in providing hikers with critical information such as route information, local attractions, and practical suggestions. In Germany, these centers are strategically positioned in major hiking locations and towns, providing extensive help to guests to guarantee a pleasant and memorable trip.

Services Offered:

- Trail Information: Tourist information centers provide comprehensive maps, brochures, and guides for local hiking routes. They include trail difficulties, anticipated durations, and important sites of interest along the routes.

- Visitors may ask about accommodation alternatives in the region, which range from hotels and guesthouses to mountain huts and campers. Tourist information centers often have up-to-date listings of lodgings.

- Tourist information centers give information on public transit choices to and from hiking sites. They provide information on rail and bus timetables, as well as any available shuttle services.

- Hikers may learn about cultural events, festivals, and recreational activities that are taking place in the area. By emphasizing local attractions, tourist centers help tourists make the most of their experience.

- **Weather and Safety Warnings:** Tourist information centers give current weather and safety warnings for the area. This information is critical for hikers who want to plan their trips and be prepared for shifting weather conditions.

Locations:

- **Major Cities:** Tourist information centers are often present in large cities and provide information on surrounding hiking options. Centers in Munich, Berlin, and Frankfurt are examples.

- **Hiking Destinations:** Dedicated tourist information centers cater exclusively to outdoor enthusiasts in hiking locations such as the Bavarian Alps, Black Forest, and Harz Mountains.

- **Rail Stations and Airports:** Many major rail stations and airports in Germany include tourist information centers that provide resources to visitors.

Online Resources:

- Tourist information centers often have official websites that provide downloadable maps, pamphlets, and digital materials. Hikers may use these internet tools to prepare ahead of time and obtain information remotely.

- Tourist information centers contain contact information, such as phone numbers and email addresses, enabling hikers to reach out with particular questions or to seek help.

Local Expertise and Knowledge:

- **Staff Assistance:** The skilled personnel at tourist information centers are acquainted with the local terrain and may provide tailored suggestions depending on hikers' interests and skills.

- **Multilingual Support:** Many tourist information centers, particularly in tourist-heavy locations, employ people who speak numerous languages, including English, making it simpler for foreign tourists to receive information.

Whether hikers are seeking route suggestions, cultural experiences, or practical information, tourist information centers serve as vital information hubs, ensuring that people have the tools they need for a memorable and well-informed hiking trip in Germany.

CONCLUSION

As our complete hiking guide in Germany comes to a close, it is clear that the nation attracts hikers with a tapestry of various landscapes, a rich cultural history, and a dedication to sustainable outdoor adventures. Germany, a hiking haven, encourages folks to go on a trip that intertwines nature, history, and self-inquiry.

When we consider the grandeur of the Bavarian Alps, the magic of the Black Forest, and the rough allure of Saxon Switzerland, we realize that Germany is more than simply a destination; it is an entire experience. The painstakingly maintained and precisely signed trail networks guide hikers through old forests, past medieval castles, and beside flourishing vineyards, showcasing the country's legendary history and present.

Hiking is strongly ingrained in German culture, not only as a physical activity but as a vital aspect of existence. The devotion to conservation reflects the appreciation for the environment, with national parks, biodiversity projects, and trash reduction efforts forming the attitude of responsible outdoor adventure. Hikers, in turn, play an important part in conserving the integrity of these environments by adhering to Leave No Trace principles and a shared duty for environmental care.

Aside from the physical landscapes, Germany's cultural and gastronomic offers enrich the hiking experience. Each path provides a trip through time and taste, from ancient cities and cultural sites to the delicious joys of traditional German food. Local festivals and events add vivid vitality to the hiking experience, enabling hikers to become more than simply spectators but active participants in the cultural fabric of the places they pass.

Practical issues, such as selecting the correct equipment and gaining access to vital resources, are found in tourist information centers, internet forums, and finely created maps and guidebooks. These tools not only give critical knowledge but also act as portals to a community of like-minded people who share a love of adventure and the great outdoors.

The echoes of footsteps and the rustling of leaves become a monument to the fundamental connection between people and the environment as the sun sets on the trails of Germany, putting a golden light on the landscapes traveled. The guide offered here is more than just a collection of facts; it is an invitation to enter a world where each route is a tale waiting to be told, each peak a victory, and each shared moment a celebration of the beauty that emerges when footsteps touch the land.

With a sense of adventure and the desire to see new places, this guide bids you farewell, certain that the routes across Germany will always inspire fresh journeys and exciting discoveries for you to come. May every hiker find an adventure instead of an objective, and may Germany's landscapes always beckon the spirit of adventure to discover, cherish, and preserve the riches that nature and culture so delicately weave together in this amazing part of the world.

Made in United States
Troutdale, OR
05/27/2024

20153178R00070